AF378424

andy pandy™

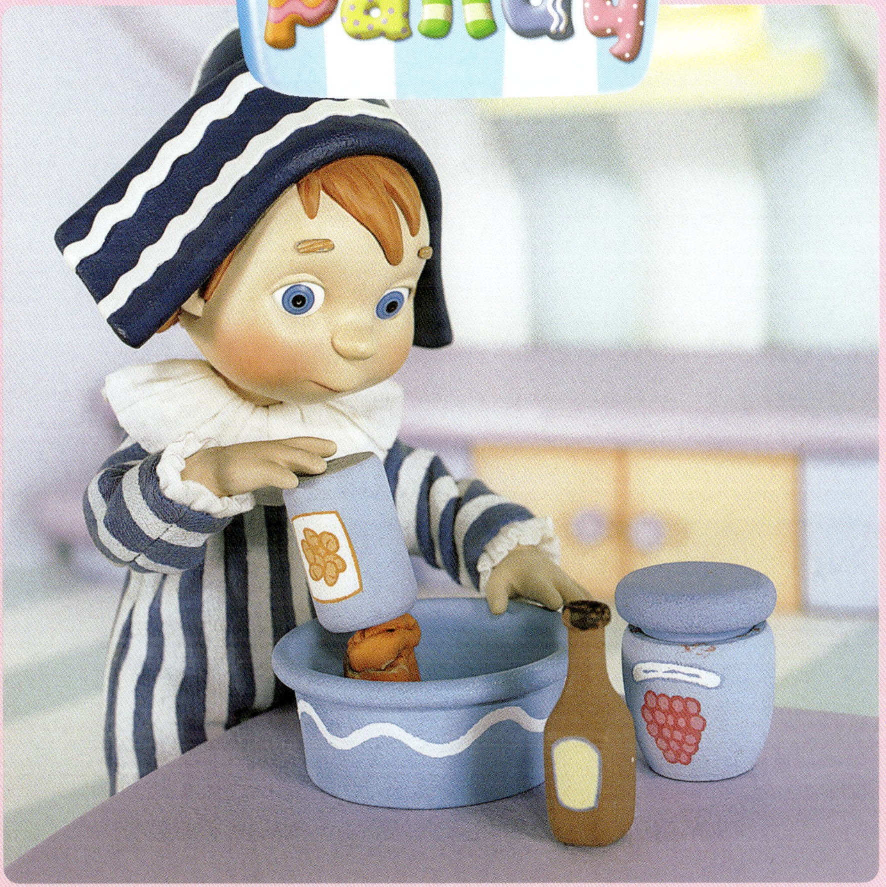

Birthday Cake

CBeebies
BBC

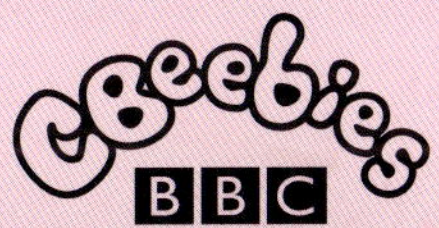

It was very early in the morning and Andy Pandy was still sound asleep.

Looby Loo tiptoed into his house and hid an envelope in Andy Pandy's cupboard.

A little later, Andy Pandy woke up
and looked in his special cupboard.
Missy Hissy came in.

Andy Pandy told
her that he didn't
know where the
envelope had
come from.

There was a birthday card inside the envelope.
They didn't know who it was for.

Andy Pandy asked Missy Hissy if she would like to have a birthday.

"Oh no!" Missy Hissy explained that whenever anyone had a birthday, they got bigger, and that she didn't want to be any longer than she already was.

Tiffo and Orbie were playing together. Andy Pandy asked Tiffo if he wanted a birthday. But the little dog barked, "No, thanks!"

So Andy Pandy asked Orbie if he would like a birthday. Orbie told Andy Pandy that he was too young to have birthdays, and bounced away.

Next, Andy Pandy saw Bilbo the sailor.
  Bilbo said that he was too old for birthdays, but offered to lend Andy Pandy some decorations if he was going to have a party.
  Andy Pandy thought that was a wonderful idea, and raced away.

Andy Pandy saw Looby Loo humming happily as she worked in her garden. He had an idea.

 Just then, Andy Pandy bumped into Teddy. He told Teddy that he was going to give Looby Loo a surprise birthday party.

Teddy thought that was a good idea. Andy Pandy said he would make the cake, and told Teddy to borrow Bilbo's decorations.

Andy Pandy had never made a cake before, but Teddy said it was easy to make an ice cream cake. All Andy Pandy needed to do was put his favourite foods into a cake tin and then put it in the freezer.

Into the cake tin went Andy Pandy's favourite things: baked beans, raspberry jam, ice cream and bananas...

...mashed potatoes and brown sauce! Soon the cake was ready to go in the freezer.

While Andy Pandy was making the cake, Tiffo decided to help Teddy with the decorations. But he just made a mess, and Teddy got cross.

Andy Pandy thought the cake must be ready.
He took it out of the freezer. It looked a little odd.

He took the cake outside and everyone agreed that
Andy Pandy's cake was very strange. But something
smelled delicious! What could it be?

Looby Loo had baked a wonderful cake. Andy Pandy stared at Looby Loo's cake and the cake stared back. It looked just like Andy Pandy!
  Looby Loo told Andy Pandy that she had put the card in his cupboard.

Then, all Andy Pandy's friends gave him cards and presents. They had known it was his birthday all along!

Then, all Andy Pandy's friends gave him cards and presents. They had Known it was his birthday all along!

Andy Pandy had lots of lovely birthday treats but, best of all, he had two very special cakes!

It was the best birthday Andy Pandy ever had, and
Looby Loo's cake was delicious!